Exploring
VALENCIA

Travel Guide 2024

A journey through culture and vibrant coastal city

Crystal F. Tanner

Copyright

Copyright © Crystal F. Tanner 2024

All rights reserved. No part of this book may be reproduced, stored in a retrieval system, or transmitted by any means, electronic, mechanical, photocopying, recording, scanning, or otherwise, without the prior written permission of the copyright owner.

Overview of Valencia

My cheeks turned gold as I ate hot paella, laughter erupting between bites. My awkward sevillana steps echoed throughout the cobblestone streets, eliciting shouts and cheeky winks. I chased sunsets through Ciudad de las Artes, where modern glass giants blushed with the setting sun. Sunbeams danced on old arches at El Carmen's heart, painting stories on worn stone. My camera sang to the fierce pulse of flamenco, catching the dancer's essence in a swirl of fabric and fire. A fleeting moment of tranquility beneath Turia's whispering leaves, Valencia's magic woven into my laughter. A promise was spoken on the breeze with each goodbye: "Hasta luego, Valencia, I'll dance to your rhythm again."

Table of contents

Welcome to Valencia — 14
   Why Visit Valencia in 2024 — 16
   What's New This Year in Valencia — 17
Getting There and Getting Around — 19
Accommodation — 32
Landmarks and Sights — 45
   The City of Arts and Sciences — 45
   Old town — 46
   Saranos Tower — 49
   Valencia Fine Arts Museum (Museu de Belles Arts de València) — 50
   Valencia cathedral — 51
   Plaza de la Virgen — 53
   Turia Gardens — 54
   Bioparc Valencia — 56
   Gulliver Park (Parque Gulliver) — 58
Delights in the Kitchen — 61
   Paella Heaven — 61
   Local cuisine — 64
   Cooking classes — 67
   Central Market — 70
   Local Tapas joint — 73
   Valencia's Sweet Treats — 77
   Classic Appeal — 77
Cultural Experience — 82
   Festivals and Events — 82
   Las Fallas — 86

Valencia International Film Festival	89
Galleries and Museums	93
Outdoor Adventures and Day Trips	**99**
Beach Vacations	99
Natural Park of Albufera	101
Sierra Calderona	105
Hiking & Nature Trails	108
Souvenirs and Shopping	**113**
Local Markets	113
Fashionable Boutiques	116
Valencia unique Souvenirs	120
Practical Suggestions	**125**
Communication and Language	125
Currency and Money matters	129
Health and Safety	132
Hospital	136
Conclusion	**140**

Map of Valencia

Exploring Valencia travel guide 2024

Itinerary Today

Day 1

morning

Start your trip to Valencia with a guided tour of Valencia's Old Town and immerse yourself in the city's rich history. Then enjoy a traditional Valencian breakfast at La Riva, renowned for its authentic flavors and cozy atmosphere.

Afternoon

In the afternoon, explore the architectural wonders of the City of Arts and Sciences (Ciudad de las Artes y las Ciencias). For lunch, enjoy the innovative cuisine of Mercatbar, a popular spot for modern Spanish cuisine.

Evening

Experience vibrant local culture on an evening tapas and drinks tour in Valencia. Enjoy a variety of tapas paired with local wines and end the evening with a flamenco show with drinks during the Valencia Flamenco Show at La Linterna.

Day 2

morning. Visit Valencia's Paella Workshop, Tapas Market and Luzafa to discover the secrets of Spain's most popular dish. Enjoy your creations and

explore the vibrant Ruzafa neighborhood. Start your day by ordering a cup of coffee at Cervecería Maipi.

Afternoon. On your way to Bioparc Valencia, take a leisurely

bike ride through the Jardí del Túria Gardens and get up close to a variety of wildlife. For lunch, visit La

Pepica, a historic restaurant famous for paella.

Evening

Grab a glass of local wine and watch the sunset on a comfortable Valencia catamaran cruise with sunset option as you sail along the coast. End the evening with a delicious dinner at La Pilareta, famous for its seafood and traditional Valencian cuisine.

Day 3
morning

Depart from futuristic hemispheric Valencia and continue with an interactive tour of the Principe Felipe Science Museum. Enjoy a quick breakfast at

Restaurante Navarro before diving into the world of science.

Afternoon

For lunch, visit the Michelin-starred restaurant at El Poblet, where the creative cuisine of Chef Quique Dacosta will delight your taste buds. Then continue your scientific exploration at the Oceanografic

(L\'Oceanogràfic), one of the largest aquariums in Europe.

Evening

Enjoy lunch at Casa Montaña, a historic bodega renowned for its wide selection of wines and delicious tapas. End the evening with a visit to the Valencia Palo Santo Flamenco Show, where the passion for flamenco comes to life.

In Valencia

Welcome to Valencia

Valencia welcomes you with wide arms, with sunshine spilling over cobblestone streets, laughter dancing on salty sea air, and the aroma of paella wafting through lively plazas. This lively Spanish city will paint your visit with colors brighter than a Fallas bonfire, whether you're a seasoned traveler or an inquisitive first-timer.

Dive into history by exploring the Barrio del Carmen's historic lanes, where Roman walls whisper stories and Gothic marvels like La Lonja de la Seda stand in timeless splendor. Climb the Miguelete tower for panoramic views, or follow the narrative of the Holy Grail through the Valencia Cathedral.

Enjoy the sun and sea: Golden beaches spread along the dazzling Mediterranean, enticing you to sunbathe, kayak through blue waves, or create sandcastles with children's laughing. Rent a bike and ride around Turia Gardens, a vibrant green paradise in the middle of the city.

Indulge in a symphony of flavors: Paella Valenciana, with its saffron-kissed rice and richness of local fish, is a must, but there are plenty of other gastronomic options. Your taste senses will tango with Spanish specialties, from tapas hopping in lively bars to Michelin-starred feasts.

Embrace the fiesta spirit: the pulse of Valencia beats to the rhythm of festivity. From the exhilarating Las Fallas festival - a frenzy of fire, music, and huge satirical puppets - to the exuberant fallas music ringing through the streets, joy and passion can be found in every corner.

Nights that dance under the stars: As the sun sets, Valencia changes into a painting of lively nightlife. Sip sangria on rooftop terraces with views of the city lights, sway to Flamenco rhythms in tiny tablaos, or get lost in the pulsating intensity of nightclubs.

Valencia, however, is more than simply views and sounds; it is the warmth of friendly grins, contagious laughter that spills from open doors, and unhurried sips of coffee on sunny squares. It's a city that will embrace you, asking you to dance to its beat, savor its flavors, and make memories that will last long after your time is over.

Why Visit Valencia in 2024

Valencia is appealing to both the eyes and the wallet. The Jard del Tria's verdant tones contrast with the beautiful golden sand and brilliant cerulean waves lapping against its shores. And the color of its oranges is as vibrant as their flavor. Those who believe this Spanish coastal city lacks charm may have never wandered beneath the blossoming citrus trees or listened to the murmur of the Valencian accent amidst the vegetable kiosks of the Mercado Central. Although it spent years in the shadows of larger cities, Valencia now provides a blend of Madrid's heritage and Barcelona's current vibe at a slightly lower cost.

What's New This Year in Valencia

Absolutely! Buckle up, because Valencia has a lot of exciting new things in store for 2024:

Valencia, the reigning European Green Capital 2024, is driving projects focused on sustainability, fair green transition, and climate neutrality. A busy program of eco-focused events, workshops, film festivals, and local initiatives aimed at lowering the city's carbon impact can be expected.

Blossoming Hortensia Herrero Art Centre: Art lovers, rejoice! The Hortensia Herrero Centre of Contemporary Art, housed within the historic Valeriola Palace, has opened its doors. Immerse yourself in Hortensia Herrero's private collection, which includes international artists like Andreas Gursky and Spanish greats like Jaume Plensa. Temporary exhibitions promise to keep the artistic spark alive.

Science Meets Pixar's Magic: Immerse yourself in the captivating world of Pixar at the "The Science of Pixar" exhibition, which is on display until October 3rd. Explore the scientific and technological wizardry that goes into generating realistic textures and dynamic movement in your favorite animated flicks. Kids (and, let's be honest, adults) will have a great time!

Beyond the New: Keep in mind that Valencia's allure extends far beyond these recent arrivals. Don't pass up iconic encounters such as:

Fallas Festival: In March, the city erupts in a blaze of inventiveness and satire as part of the world-famous Fallas festival. Giant satirical puppets (ninots) tower over the streets before exploding in a fiery conclusion.

City of Arts and Sciences: Explore the City of Arts and Sciences complex's futuristic architecture and amazing displays. Explore the Oceanogràfic aquarium, and the Hemisfèric IMAX cinema, or take a stroll through the tranquil Umbracle.

Getting There and Getting Around

Airports

Valencia has one main airport, which is strategically positioned for quick access to the city center and beyond. So, pack your bags and prepare to take off - here's all you need to know about Valencia Airport:

Officially known as Aeropuerto de Valencia-Manises (VLC), it serves as the city's major air gateway, handling both domestic and international flights. The airport, which is only 8 kilometers west of Valencia in the municipality of Manises, is easily accessible by a variety of modes of transportation:

Metro: Metrovalencia Lines 3 and 5 will take you directly to the city center in about 20 minutes, making it a speedy and economical choice.

Bus: Fernanbus and ALSA run regular bus services connecting the airport to the city center and other surrounding areas.

Taxis are readily accessible outside the airport 24 hours a day, seven days a week, and provide a convenient and pleasant transport to your destination.

Car rental: Major car rental firms have counters at the airport, allowing you to rent a vehicle for your exploration of the city and beyond.

Valencia International Airport has two passenger terminals:

Terminal 1: Handles mostly domestic and some European aircraft.

Terminal 2: Is primarily used for foreign flights, however, it also handles some domestic routes.

Both terminals provide a variety of amenities and services, such as:

- Duty-free purchases
- Cafes and restaurants
- Currency conversion
- ATMs

- Storage for luggage
- Tourist information offices
- Free Wi-Fi is available.

Here are some more details about Valencia Airport:

- It is Spain's tenth busiest airport and the Valencian Community second busiest.
- In 2019, it served nearly 8.5 million passengers.
- The airport serves approximately 120 destinations in Europe, Africa, and the Middle East.
- It is well-known for its efficient operations and cutting-edge facilities.

Train Transportation

When it comes to train travel in Valencia, you have a lot of options! The city has two distinct rail stations, each serving various travel needs and providing unique experiences. Buckle up and join us as we journey through the world of Valencian train stations:

Estació del Nord

The City Centre Jewel: Built in 1917, this magnificent Art Nouveau beauty serves as Valencia's main train station. It's a perfect starting point for visiting Valencia because it's directly in the heart of the city, near the Plaza de Toros, and within walking distance of key sites like the Cathedral and Central Market.

Regional Connections: Estació del Nord principally serves as a center for regional trains (cercanas), which connect Valencia to adjacent towns and cities like as Ganda, Mogente, and Castellón de la Plana. Day trips or touring the Valencian region are ideal.

National Attractions: Despite its regional concentration, Estació del Nord also provides connections to other Spanish cities like Barcelona, Madrid, and Pamplona by long-distance trains such as Alaris and Euromed.

A feast for the senses: Estació del Nord is a feast for the senses in addition to its transportation purpose. Admire the magnificent architecture, stroll through the bustling ticket hall, and sample local fare at the on-site cafes and restaurants.

Joaquin Sorolla station

High-Speed Haven: For those looking for a quick getaway, Joaquin Sorolla Station, located around 4 kilometers from the city center, is your gateway to high-speed AVE trains. Travel to Madrid in 1.5 hours or explore southern Spain via links to Albacete and Cuenca.

Modern convenience: Sorolla Station, built in 2010, is a tribute to modern design and efficiency. Enjoy spacious waiting areas, a diverse selection of shops and restaurants, and close access to public transport such as Metro and taxi ranks.

Beyond Trains: If you arrive on an AVE train, the station has a free shuttle bus service to Estació del Nord, making it easy to access the city center. Additionally, rental car firms operate on-site desks, making it easy to explore the region.

Bus Transportation

Valencia's buses are colorful companions on your journey across the city and beyond, weaving a vivid network across the urban landscape. Whether you're a seasoned bus passenger or a curious novice, get ready to board and experience Valencia's efficient and comfortable public transit system.

A Network That Goes Everywhere:

EMT Valencia operates the city bus network, which has over 150 routes linking every nook and crevice of Valencia and going out to surrounding cities. From bustling avenues to lovely villages, a bus is waiting to take you there.

Diverse Routes, Diverse Needs

Urban Lines: These bright orange buses are your ticket to exploring the city. They cover all districts, key sites, and residential areas, allowing you to easily reach your destination. Look for route numbers that begin with a number, such as line 19, which connects the City of Arts and Sciences to the seashore.

Interurban Lines: Beyond the City Limits? Green buses with "Metrobus" branding transport you to adjacent towns such as Sagunto, Paterna, and Torrent. Ideal for day excursions or getting away from the city.

Night buses: Don't be concerned about late-night bus rides! From 10:30 p.m. to 2:00 a.m. on weekdays and 3:30 a.m. on weekends, special blue-colored buses operate on particular routes, assuring safe and convenient overnight travel.

How to Board Like a Pro

Signal your stop: Unlike in several places, there is no automatic stop request mechanism. Simply extend your arm at any marked bus stop to hail a bus.

Front door entry: Enter through the front door, exit through the back: Board through the front door, validate your ticket or card and find your seat. Exit the ship through the back doors.

Tickets and Payments: There are numerous options! Single tickets can be purchased on board (pay exact change or use the EMTicket app) or rechargeable travel cards like Suma or Bonobus can be purchased in advance at kiosks, tobacco shops, or EMT offices.

Tools for a Smooth Journey

EMTic App: Your digital pocket guide, the EMTic App! For real-time bus arrival information, route planning, and ticket purchases, download the EMT Valencia app.

Bus stop: Look for bright orange bus stop signs with route numbers and timetables. Many stops also have electronic screens that display real-time arrival information.

Beyond the Fundamentals

Accessibility: All buses have low-floor access and specific spaces for wheelchairs and strollers.

Valencia prioritizes environmentally friendly efforts, with hybrid and electric buses rapidly joining the fleet.

Sustainability efforts: Drivers prioritize passenger safety, so be seated while the bus is going and hold on to the railings if you are standing.

So, get on board and experience Valencia's dynamic pulse from the comfort of a bus! Remember, with a little forethought and these helpful hints, you'll be navigating the city like a local in no time. Good luck on your journey! (Have a safe journey!)

Vehicle rentals

Buckle up for a fantastic adventure into the world of Valencia car rentals! Whether you're looking for a quick city cruiser or a reliable horse for touring sun-kissed beaches and lovely villages, Valencia has a plethora of alternatives to fuel your Valencian journey.

A Wheel Spectrum

Global giant: Renowned brands such as Hertz, Avis, Europcar, and Sixt have a significant presence in Valencia, offering a wide choice of vehicles at various pricing points, from modest city cars to luxury SUVs. Expect dependable service and familiar convenience, which is great for frequent travelers.

Local Charmers: Don't underestimate the unsung heroes of your community! Smaller rental firms, such as Centauro, Goldcar, and Ok Mobility, frequently advertise low pricing and courteous service. They may have a smaller fleet, but they frequently include extra bonuses such as full insurance or unlimited mileage, making them cost-effective options.

Two-Wheeled Adventures: Feeling daring? Explore Valencia by bike! Scooter and motorcycle rentals are becoming increasingly popular, providing a fun and easy way to explore the city and its surrounding coastline. Just remember to wear a helmet and follow all traffic laws.

Location Location Location:

Airport Advantage: The majority of major car rental companies have counters at Valencia Airport, allowing you to pick up your wheels as soon as you arrive. Ideal for reducing wait times and maximizing vacation time.

Convenience in the City Centre: There are numerous rental companies distributed throughout the city center, providing simple access if you are already established in your accommodation. This option allows you to compare prices and locate the best car for your needs.

Price and point and perks

Shop Around: Prices can vary greatly, so compare rates from various companies before making a decision. Online booking systems can assist you in locating the finest rates.

Think beyond the price tag: Consider variables such as insurance coverage, mileage constraints, fuel policies, and additional fees before making a decision. A higher price can sometimes include important additions that provide peace of mind.

Understand Your Requirements: Match your car to your plan. Choose a compact car for city cruising, an SUV for rough terrain exploration, or a minivan for family outings.

Tips for a Smooth Renting Experience

Plan Ahead: To avoid disappointment and to obtain the best rates, book your car in advance, especially during peak season.

Bring the essential: Any Bring a valid driver's license, passport, and credit card for verification.

Read the Small Print: Fully comprehend the rental agreement, including insurance coverage, fuel policies, and cancellation fines.

Inspect the Before driving away, inspect the vehicle for any existing damage and document it.

Museum of art and galleries Museu de Belles Arts de València)

Accommodation

Hotels in Various Districts

1. Malcolm and Barret Hotels

The Malcolm & Barrett Hotel is 5 5-minute' walk from the City of Arts and Sciences. It contains 168 comfortable single, double, and triple rooms with air conditioning (hot/cold), free wifi, a 40-inch LED TV with international channels, a safe, a magnifying mirror, a desk, a bathroom with Shower, hairdryer, toiletries. Visit our kids' room, where they will have a blast. Board games, stories to read, books to color, a large blackboard to express their creativity, and a play station for the most avid video game players. The hotel Malcom & Barret has a restaurant with a buffet breakfast, lunch, and dinner a la carte, as well as a gin bar for a drink after a day of work or touring. It also has meeting or event spaces, a 24-hour front desk, and luggage storage. The hotel's position provides it a great starting point for exploring both the city center and the beach, as well as the Congress Palace neighborhood. Parking is not advised for cars longer than 4.5 meters.

Room characteristics

Blackout drapes

The use of air conditioning

Desk

Housekeeping

Safe

TV with a flat-screen

Shower with a door

Toiletries are provided at no cost.

Location

Avenida Ausias March 59, Valencia, Spain 46013

2. Hotel krammer

Travellers' Favourite

Hotel Kramer is located next to the Congress Palace and has 70 rooms, all of which are decorated elegantly and modernly on the outside and are equipped with cold/hot air conditioning, the latest generation LED TV with international channels, free WI-FI and a fully equipped bathroom with shower, hairdryer, and amenities. It also has a

24-hour reception, a daily cleaning service, cots on request, and a one-time airport transfer fee. The hotel features a cafeteria/restaurant called "Kram Bar" where you can enjoy our buffet a la carte breakfast, a Mediterranean cuisine menu, or have a drink while watching the major sporting events on the huge screen. Check-in begins at 2 p.m. Check-out time: noon Important: This property does not accept bookings from student groups or bachelor/stag parties.

Room characteristics

Soundproof rooms

The use of air conditioning

Housekeeping

Safe

Refrigerator

TV with a flat-screen

Location

Avenida Campanar 90, Valencia, Spain 46015

3. Hotel Las Arenas Balneario Ressort

The architecture of the Las Arenas Spa Resort Hotel, the first 5-star Deluxe hotel in the Valencia region, has been carefully considered such that it opens out onto the sea in Valencia. This hotel, only a few minutes walk from the city center, has a wonderful location on Las Arenas beachfront, with views of the sea. The majority of the 253 rooms and suites offer bathrooms with hydromassage cabins and baths, plasma TV with satellite, WiFi Internet connection, and CD player. Most rooms also have wide terraces with views of the Mediterranean Sea.

Room characteristics

The use of air conditioning

Additional loo

Housekeeping

Personal balcony

Room service is available.

Minibar

Refrigerator

TV with a flat-screen

Location

Eugenia Viñes 22-24, Valencia, Spain

4. Cosmo Hotel and Bar

Cosmo Hotel Boutique is a designed hotel with a restaurant bar in the heart of Valencia, 700 meters from the North Train Station. This 3-star hotel offers a tour desk as well as luggage storage. A 24-hour front desk, airport shuttle service, concierge service, and free WiFi are available throughout the property.

The hotel's rooms include a desk, a flat-screen TV, a private bathroom, bed linen and towels. Each room includes a wardrobe and a kettle.

Breakfast is Available à la carte au Cosmo Hotel Boutique.

Nearby attractions include San Nicolás Church, Turia Gardens, and the González Mart National Museum of Ceramics and Decorative Arts. Valencia Airport is 8 kilometers away from Cosmo Hotel Boutique

Room characteristics

Blackout drapes

Soundproof rooms

The use of air conditioning

Housekeeping

There are interconnected rooms available.

Kettle, electric

TV with a flat-screen

Shower with a door

Location

Valencia, Spain, Calle Maria Cristina 8, 46001

5. The Westin Valencia.

Room characteristics

The use of air conditioning

Housekeeping

Personal balcony

Room service is available.

Safe

Minibar

Refrigerator

TV with a flat-screen

Location

Valencia, Spain, Calle Amadeo de Saboya 16, 46010.

009 1 844-631-0595

6. Hotel Meliá Valencia

The Melia Valencia is located near the Congress Centre on the Avenida de les Corts Valencianes, in one of Valencia's most important and dynamic areas. The hotel has a spectacular Convention Centre among its magnificent facilities. All of the rooms are spacious, bright, and open to the outside. Melia Valencia is an excellent choice for both business and leisure travelers due to its excellent location in the city center, comfortable, well-equipped rooms, and superior service quality. The hotel has a pool that is open seasonally!

Room characteristics

Blackout drapes

Bathrobes

The use of air conditioning

Housekeeping

Minibar

TV via cable or satellite

Beds that are extra long

Toiletries are provided at no cost.

Location

Avenida Cortes Valencianas 52, Valencia, Spain 46015

6. Vincci mercat

The Hotel Vincci Mercat 4* is a newly built building in one of Valencia's most sought-after tourist areas. Its location near the recently renovated Central Market, City Hall, and Plaza de Espana is ideal for those who want to walk around the city and enjoy one of the city's main shopping districts. Enjoy a hotel in the heart of Valencia with a rooftop pool where you can sunbathe. The pool bar is only open during the season. The pool measures 5.70 m x 3.70 m and has a depth of 1.10 m.

Room characteristics

Blackout drapes

The use of air conditioning

Desk

Housekeeping

Room service is available.

Maker of coffee or tea

TV with a flat-screen

Toiletries are provided at no cost.

Location

Valencia, Spain, Calle Linterna 31, 46001

8. Vincci Lys

The hotel is located in the heart of Valencia, just a two-minute walk from the train station and the Town Hall Square. Vincci Lys Hotel is set on a quiet pedestrian street surrounded by a variety of shops, restaurants, and culturally significant buildings. Decorated stylishly and appealingly. It is the only hotel in Valencia's center with a parking lot and direct access to its grounds.

Room characteristics

Blackout drapes

The use of air conditioning

Desk

Housekeeping

Personal balcony

Minibar

TV with a flat-screen

Toiletries are provided at no cost.

Location

Valencia, Spain, Calle Martinez Cubells 5, 46002.

9. NH Valencia Centre

The NH Valencia Centre is located in the heart of Valencia, close to a multitude of attractions and the main bus station. The hotel is close to a cultural, business, and recreational region.

Room characteristics

Housekeeping

Room service is available.

Safe

TV with a flat-screen

Different sorts of rooms

Wedding suite

Non-smoking rooms are available.

Suites

Location

Valencia, Spain, Calle de Ricardo Mico 1, 46009

Name and address in the native language

009 1 212-245-5462

10. Eurostar Gran Valencia

Discover why Eurostars Gran Valencia is the hotel of choice for many visitors to Valencia. It offers a family-friendly atmosphere with an array of amenities geared for travelers like you, providing a great balance of value, comfort, and convenience.

Eurostars Gran Valencia Hotel is a short distance from Barrio del Carmen (1.3 mi) and Parroquia de San Nicolás de Bari y San Pedro Mártir (1.5 km) for visitors interested in viewing popular monuments while in Valencia.

The rooms have a flat-screen TV, air conditioning, and a minibar, and you can stay connected with complimentary wifi, allowing you to rest and recharge with ease.

The Eurostars Gran Valencia Hotel has a front desk that is open 24 hours a day, a rooftop patio, and a concierge. In addition, as a valued Eurostars Gran Valencia Hotel guest, you will have access to an on-site pool and poolside bar. Parking is available for guests arriving by car.

If you're in Valencia, enjoy some ramen at one of the neighboring eateries, such as Kamon, Ramen Kuma, or Ryukishin Valencia.

If time allows, a popular destination within walking distance is Jardi del Turia.

Room characteristics

Hotel_amenity_soundproof_rooms

Air_conditioning

Desk

Interconnected_rooms_available

Room_service

Minibar

Flatscreen_tv

Whirlpool_bathtub

Location

Valencia, Spain, Calle Valle de Ayora 3, 46015

Catedral De Valencia

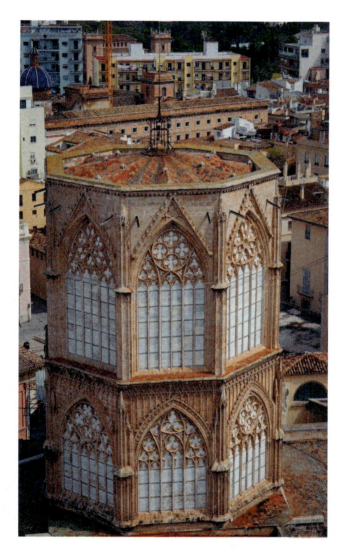

Landmarks and Sights

The City of Arts and Sciences

For its futuristic design, the Ciutat de les Arts y las Ciències (also known as the City of Arts and Sciences) is a traveler's favorite. The museum's contemporary architecture (by Santiago Calatrava) houses the Museu de les Ciències (a science museum), the Hemisfèric (a planetarium and IMAX theatre), the Oceanogràfic (Europe's largest aquarium), and the Palau de les Arts Reina Sofa (a performing arts venue), among other attractions.

Previous visitors praised the complex's numerous options and advised wearing comfortable shoes; the site is so large (approximately 452,000 square feet) that you'll be doing a lot of walking. Reviewers suggested allocating an afternoon, or possibly two to three days, to see the full complex. Visitors laud the science museum for its interactive exhibits and the aquarium for its gorgeous design.

The City of Arts and Sciences is open every day (except Christmas Day), though hours vary based on the season. It is generally open daily from 10 a.m. until 6, 7, or 9 p.m. You can buy individual attraction tickets or a combo ticket that gives you admission to various places. Adult admission to the Museu de les Ciències, for example, is roughly 8.70 euros (or around $9.50). Access to the full complex is 44.20 euros (about $48) for up to three days. To get to the complex, take the metro line 10 to Ciutat Arts and Sciències-Justicia Alameda; you can also take buses 13, 15, 25, 35, 95, and 99.

Old town

The Ciutat Vella, or Old Town, is a lively mix of historical sites, bars, and restaurants located within the medieval city walls. This UNESCO-listed zone contains over 2,000 years of history, and many of the top attractions are conveniently located nearby. Valencia Cathedral, the city hall, the Central

Market, and the Silk Exchange are among them, as are various exhibitions of bright street art. While the historic city walls have been destroyed by time and urban expansion, the Serranos Towers and Torres de Quart (fortified city gates) remain as markers.

Previous visitors praised the historical sites, picturesque lanes, and souvenir shops. They also like the nightlife (it is the city's most vibrant region) and the diversity of restaurants.

Even though this district is divided into six neighborhoods, you can easily walk from one end of the Old Town to the other in 20 minutes. Walking or biking is the easiest method to navigate the small historic streets. You can take a self-directed tour, a guided walking trip, or a Segway or bicycle tour. Because of the old architecture, there are no metro stops in the Ciutat Vella district, although you can walk there from Turia (line 1), Alameda, Angel Guimera (lines 1, 3 and 5), Xativa (lines 3 and 5), and Colon (lines 3 and 5). Similarly, while bus routes do not cover most of the Old Town, numerous lines do skirt the perimeter.

Old town Map

Saranos Tower

The Serranos Towers are remnants of Valencia's long-gone city walls. They were built in 1392 as a defensive construction around the city gates and served as an aristocratic prison from 1586 to 1887. They are now an iconic Valencian landmark and one of only two extant towers of its type in the city. Climb the old steps for panoramic views of the city and the Turia River. Crowds assemble at the foot of the towers to witness a fireworks show during the Fallas festival.

The Valencian Gothic architecture, as well as the handy position (only a stone's throw from the Valencia Cathedral), were commended by visitors. Some visitors warned that because there are no handrails, climbing the towers is not suitable for little children, but most believed the vistas were worth it.

The Serranos Towers are open from 10 a.m. to 7 p.m., Tuesday through Saturday. to 2 p.m. and beginning at 3 p.m. to 7 p.m. On Sundays and holidays, the store opens at 10 a.m. to 2 p.m. The towers, however, are closed for safety concerns during inclement weather, as well as on Christmas, New Year's, Three Kings, and May 1. Depending on the time of day, they may close significantly earlier in the winter. The towers are easily accessible by foot or bicycle from the Old Town. Admission is 2 euros (about $2) for adults and 1 euro (about $1) for children aged 7 to 12. The towers are free to view on Sundays.

Valencia Fine Arts Museum (Museu de Belles Arts de València)

If you like Spanish artists like Velázquez, Goya, and El Greco, don't miss the free Museu de Belles Arts, which also contains a large collection of medieval paintings, with a focus on religious art and relics. Approximately 2,000 paintings and statues, some dating back to the 14th century, are among its collections. The structure is also extremely interesting. It was previously the Seminary College of Saint Pius V, which was founded in the 17th century.

Recent visitors praised the diverse range of artistic genres on show. However, other people say it's not a must-see unless you're interested in Spanish artists with a focus on religious art.

The museum is located on the Turia River's northern bank. You may get there by metro (Alameda) or bus (Nos. 6, 11, 16, 26, 94, 95 C2).

The nearest metro stations are Alameda and Pont de Fusta. The museum is open from 10am to 5pm, Tuesday through Sunday. except on Christmas and New Year's Day, till 8 p.m. Admission is free.

Valencia cathedral

The Valencia Cathedral, located in Plaza de la Reina, is arguably best known for its claim to possess the Holy Grail. The cathedral was built on the site of a former mosque in 1262 and features a variety of architectural styles, including Romanesque, Baroque, and Gothic.

Visitors in the past were thrilled with the cathedral's interior, albeit some complained about the entrance cost. Others praised the audio guide that comes with admittance, saying it gave valuable historical background. There are audio guides available in several languages, including English.

Except from November to March, when it is only accessible for half days on Sundays, the cathedral is open daily. Hours vary depending on the season, but the cathedral normally opens at 10 a.m. Monday through Saturday. Depending on the day and season, it is open until as late as 6:30 p.m. It welcomes guests beginning at 2 p.m. on Sundays when it is open. The cathedral and its museum cost 9 euros (about $9.50) to enter. The Gothic Miguelete Tower, which offers spectacular views of the city, costs around 2.50 euros (around $2.75). The cathedral is accessible via bus lines 4, 9, 19, 81, 94, C1 and C2.

Plaza de la Virgen

The marble-floored Plaza de la Virgen, adjacent to the Valencia Cathedral, is a great place to people-watch and admire some of the city's architecture. From here, one can see the Gothic Valencia Cathedral (where the chalice from the Last Supper is claimed to be kept) as well as the Baroque Real Basilica de Nuestra Seora de los Desamparados, which has pink walls and blue roof tiles.

The stunning Tria Fountain, which portrays the Turia River and has statues of eight ladies pouring water from pitchers, as well as a colossal sculpture of Neptune seated atop the fountain, are other areas of interest. Every Thursday at noon, the Tribunal de las Aguas meets outside the Door of the Apostles, carrying on a 1,000-year-old tradition. The Water Tribunal is made up of eight farmers clothed in black who sit in a circle and negotiate water access to the orchards (in Valencian). From the perspective of tourists, this scenario is a strange spectacle.

Many shops and restaurants surround the area, which is littered with tables and chairs spilling out from cafes and bars and is usually visited by a variety of street performers, Of course, the popular plaza is always open, and some visitors find it especially appealing at night. If you want to avoid crowds, avoid visiting on a weekend afternoon in the afternoon.

Turia Gardens

The Jard del Tria (or Garden of the Turia) may appear strange to strangers, as it boasts more than a dozen bridges designed to span a river that no longer exists. Jard del Tria, one of the country's greatest urban parks, was established in the aftermath of a fatal Turia River flood in 1957, which was later diverted throughout the mid-to-late 1960s. The gardens now include orange and palm trees, as well as rose bushes, amid a diverse diversity of vegetation. Cafes, football (soccer) pitches, children's play areas, rugby pitches, fountains, baseball diamonds, running tracks, skate parks, and miniature golf courses are all available at the park. The park is unsurprisingly popular with runners and cyclists. It is also great for families with children.

Recent visitors praise the green space for the variety of activities available as well as the tranquil ambiance.

The Jard del Tria, at approximately 270 acres in size, winds its way past many of Valencia's other top attractions, including the City of Arts and Sciences (Ciutat de les Arts y les Ciències), the Valencian Institute of Modern Art (Institut Valencià d'Art Modern), Gulliver Park, and the Torres de Serranos. The region is accessible via metro lines 3, 5, 7, and 9, as well as several bus routes. The garden is open 24 hours a day, 365 days a year.

Bioparc Valencia

The Bioparc Valencia is a 25-acre zoo located in the city's northwest. This isn't just any zoo, though; it's an immersion zoo, which means it removes or conceals many of the boundaries that traditional zoos erect between different species, including humans. Species that naturally (and safely) coexist in the wild are placed together, while other gentle species, such as lemurs, are free to interact with humans face to face. Other roadblocks are simply buried to give tourists the impression that they are in the wilderness, which is a particular delight for recent visitors. The park's goal is to reproduce the African continent, with zebras, Nile crocodiles, giraffes, and elephants scattered among four major ecosystems.

Previous visitors appreciated the opportunity to see the animals up close and thought the unique arrangement was an interesting break from the typical zoo. Remember the Bioparc's animal rules: they should not be touched or fed, and they should not be disturbed by yelling or flash photography. Aside from that, employ common sense: don't jump over the fence to meet the tigers.

Reviewers advised allotting two to three hours to see the attraction.

Bioparc Valencia is open daily beginning at 10 a.m. till 6 p.m.; during the summer, it is open until 8 p.m. To get to the zoo, walk along the Turia riverbed in the direction of Parque de Cabecera or take metro lines 3, 5, or 9 to the Nou d'Octubre stop. The Bioparc can also be reached by bus lines 67, 73, 95, 98, and 99. Admission to the zoo costs roughly 26.90 euros (approximately $29) for adults and approximately 21 euros (approximately $23) for children aged 4 to 12. Children under 3 can enter for free. There are various restaurants and a playground on-site.

Gulliver Park (Parque Gulliver)

If a park named after the giant from Jonathan Swift's "Gulliver's Travels" sounds fantastical, that's because it is. However, Gulliver Park is more than just a literary tribute; it's a playground comprised of numerous slides and staircases arranged in the shape of its prone namesake. The figure's hat has a small version of Gulliver drawn on it, so you can get an idea of what the giant character looks like when viewed from above.

The park is popular with children, although some adults appreciate the mention of bookworms. However, adults will appreciate the newly renovated facilities, due in November 2022, including safety ropes at the edges of the steepest slopes and soft floor surfaces.

Recent visitors warn the slides can get hot in the Valencian sun, and to expect your kids to go home dusty, but happy.

The park is located within Jard del Tria and is free to attend; its hours vary by season, but it normally opens at 10 a.m. and shuts about 8 p.m. during spring and summer (with a siesta break during July and August) and around 5:30 p.m. during winter. when the weather is cooler

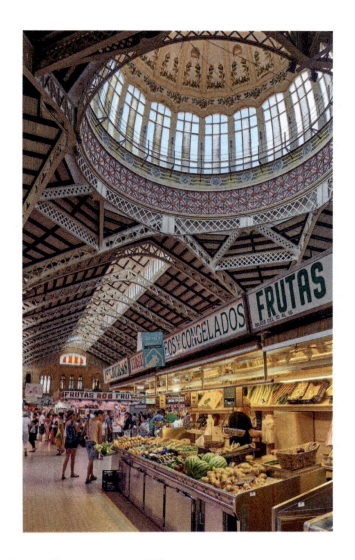

Delights in the Kitchen

Paella Heaven

Valencia's streets virtually scream "paella" at you - it's a birthright, a symphony of saffron-kissed rice, and a culinary experience just waiting to happen. But where can you locate your paella heaven amid this delectable chaos? Don't worry, paella pilgrim, for this guide will lead you through the hot landscape of Valencia's paella havens:

The Greatest Hits

La Pepica: A Valencian gastronomic legend, La Pepica lies oceanfront, waves serenading its open-air tables. Paella Valenciana, brimming with chicken, rabbit, garrofón beans, and the soul of tradition, is a must-try. It's a Valencian institution, so make a reservation.

Valencia's La Pepica

Casa Carmela: Another well-known name, Casa Carmela conjures up warm feelings and family delicacies. Their Paella Valenciana, cooked over a wood fire in a large communal pan, is pure love on a plate. Witness the miracle of paella-making and savor every delectable grain.

Casa Carmela Valencia

L'Albufera: Get away from the city and visit L'Albufera Natural Park. At Casa To David, dine on paella made right on the lagoon's edge with seafood so fresh it virtually leaps from the water. Take in the scenery, the wind, and the paella joy.

The Turns & Twists

Casa Elias: Looking for something different? With their "Paella Negra," a mesmerizing combination of rice saturated with squid ink, shellfish, and the essence of the sea, Casa Elas reinvents the paella landscape. Prepare to be amazed, as well as slightly stained - in the best conceivable manner.

Casa Elias Valencia

Paella Valenciana a Banda: For something a little different, try "Paella a Banda," a seafood-only feast brimming with mussels, prawns, squid, and the salty kiss of the Mediterranean. Try it at Els Sorells Restaurant, and remember to lap up the soup with crusty bread - proper paella etiquette!

Audrey's Kitchen: Looking for a modern twist? Audrey's Kitchen creates gourmet paellas using unusual ingredients such as duck confit, foie gras, and truffle shavings. Prepare for a magnificent (and costly) paella experience that defies convention.

Beyond the Restaurants

Central Market: Explore the busy Central Market, which is a treasure trove of fresh local ingredients. Pick up the best bomba rice, colorful vegetables, and plump sausages, then return to your Airbnb and unleash your inner Valencian chef. Remember, nothing beats a home-cooked paella!

Central Market Valencia

Cooking Classes: Take a cooking class to learn the skill of creating paella. Local specialists will teach you the secrets of fire, saffron, and bomba rice. Who knows, you might just come home a paella expert, ready to wow your friends and family.

Local cuisine

Valencia's indigenous cuisine emerges like a vivid tapestry of flavors, reflecting the sun-kissed region and the Mediterranean heartbeat of the city, beyond the sizzling, saffron-soaked beauty of paella. This guide to Valencian culinary treasures will tantalize your taste buds:

Rice is the King

Paella Valenciana: This rice dish sings with chicken, rabbit, garrofón beans, and the romance of saffron. Every Valencian family has a treasured recipe, and there are innumerable versions in restaurants, each embodying the character of the city.

Arroz a Banda: Mussels, prawns, squid, and the salty kiss of the sea combine to produce a symphony of flavors in this paella variation. With each bite, immerse yourself in the wealth of the Mediterranean.

Arrs del Senyoret: For a sumptuous twist, try "Arrs del Senyoret," which features peeled shellfish such as prawns, lobster, and clams in a saffron-infused broth, ready to be savored without messy shells.

Beyond the Rice Paddies

Esgarrat: This light salad combines roasted red peppers, onions, fish, and olives in a simple olive oil and vinegar dressing. Ideal as a tapas appetizer or a light summer lunch.

Bunyols: These scrumptious fritters are available in sweet and savory varieties, with pumpkin and aniseed in the former and cod or prawns in the latter. Put them in your mouth as if they were sunshine-flavored bites.

Fartons: These oblong pastries, a Valencian delicacy, mix nicely with horchata, a sweet tiger nut milk. Dip one end into the milky bliss, soak it, and eat!

All I pebre: Garlic and hot red peppers take center stage in this scorching meal, which is frequently served with roasted artichokes or fish. Prepare for a flavor explosion and lingering warmth.

From the Land and the Sea

L'Olleta: A Valencian comfort cuisine full of chickpeas, white beans, veggies, and pork, this substantial stew is ideal for winter evenings. Every spoonful contains the flavors of tradition.

Clóchinas: Steamed or cooked in white wine, these Valencian mussels are a delightful treat. Soak up the garlicky broth with crusty bread and let the sea wind take your cares away.

Turrón: A Valencian Christmas tradition, this delightful nougat is prepared with honey, egg whites, and almonds. But who says you can't enjoy all year? Choose your favorite flavor variety - from traditional to chocolate-infused - and enjoy the sweetness of life.

Don't Forget

Tapas Tour: Explore the lively world of Valencian tapas bars. Bites like patatas bravas, croquetas, and local cheeses are served with a glass of sangria or a cool cerveza.

Central Market: Take in the sights and sounds of the lively Central Market. Pick up fresh supplies for your culinary adventures or stop by one of the many stalls for a quick snack.

Local Wine: Enjoy exquisite Valencian wines from the regions of Utiel-Requena and Terra Alta. Find hidden jewels at small bodegas or enjoy a glass at a delightful tapas bar.

Cooking classes

The aroma of boiling paella hangs heavily in the air in Valencia, luring hungry travelers and gourmet enthusiasts alike. But what if you could avoid the crowds and discover the mysteries of this Valencian treasure for yourself? This is where the exciting world of Valencia cooking lessons comes in!

Valencia provides a buffet of cooking experiences sure to fire your kitchen passion, from ancient wisdom passed down through generations to modern interpretations of classic dishes. Here are some of the scrumptious alternatives that await you:

Traditional champion:

My first paella: Immerse yourself in the heart of Ruzafa Market, a bustling oasis for fresh vegetables and local treasures, for My First Paella. You'll master the art of paella Valenciana under the tutelage of skilled hosts, learning every step from selecting the proper rice to attaining that delicious golden crust. Bonus points for touring the market and filling up on local delicacies afterward!

Valencia Club Cocina: This delightful cooking school in the Carmen district offers private sessions packed with humor and learning. Hone your paella talents with other foodies, studying traditional techniques and savoring the fruits (or rather, rice) of your labor in a cosy communal atmosphere.

Casa Carmela: Discover the secrets of their famed wood-fired paella Valenciana at this Valencian culinary institution. Witness the magic firsthand as experienced chefs take you through the process, passing down years of knowledge and guaranteeing you leave with a paella prowess that will surprise all your friends back home.

Aside from Paella:

Travelling Spoon: Get out of town and explore the culinary traditions of the Valencian countryside. This one-of-a-kind experience transports you to a quaint family house in El Palmar, where you'll learn to make real paella Valenciana over an open fire, surrounded by the natural splendor of the Albufera Natural Park. A full taste of Valencian culture and cuisine awaits you!

Eatwith: Looking for a more personalized touch? Through Eatwith, you can connect with passionate local cooks and take an intimate cooking class in their homes. The possibilities are boundless, from traditional paella versions to modern tapas experiences. As you prepare wonderful dishes together, immerse yourself in local culture and discussion.

Horta Viva: At Horta Viva, a magnificent organic farm just outside of Valencia, embrace the farm-to-table mentality. Learn how to grow fresh ingredients and then use them to make delightful dishes such as paella Valenciana and traditional gazpacho. This eco-friendly culinary tour is ideal for individuals looking for a sustainable and immersive culinary excursion.

Central Market

Central Market! It's a Valencia symphony of colors, scents, and vivid mayhem, not just a market. Buckle up, because we're about to dive into the core of this architectural, culinary, and cultural treasure:

A Visual Delight

Modernista masterpiece: Built in 1928, the market is a Modernista masterpiece with Art Nouveau architecture. Stained glass windows dance with sunshine, and ceramic azulejos tiles weave bright stories throughout the walls. It's a photogenic location, so bring your camera!

Valencia Central Market Architecture

A Colourful Kaleidoscope: Get ready to be stunned by a rainbow of fruits and veggies. It's a feast for the eyes even before you reach for your money, with towering pyramids of oranges, flaming red peppers, emerald green artichokes, and luscious purple figs.

A Gastronomic Paradise:

Paella Paradise: The soul food of Valencia takes the stage here. Bomba rice, fresh seafood, delicate chicken, and plump sausages abound among the stalls - everything you need to make your paella masterpiece at home.

Mercado Central Valencia paella ingredients

Beyond the Paella: Don't be boxed in! The market is a gourmet feast. Local cheeses, cured meats, unusual spices, fragrant herbs, and handcrafted breads will tempt any pallet.

Second heaven: Valencia's proximity to the sea is reflected in the gleaming displays of freshly caught fish and seafood. Clams, oysters, prawns, and lobsters virtually demand to be snatched up for a delectable seafood paella or a sizzling plancha grill session.

A Cultural Experience

Chatter and Smiles: The market is alive and well. Vendors joke with customers, laughter blends with the rhythmic chopping of knives, and the air hums with the Valencian energy. Immerse yourself in the atmosphere and soak up the charm of the locals.

A Taste of Tradition: The market is more than simply a place to buy food; it's also a cultural landmark. Generations of Valencians have wandered these aisles, passing down culinary traditions and sharing stories over fresh produce baskets. Be a part of that history!

Tips for Getting Around the Market

Come Hungry: The aroma of spices and sizzling sausages will make your tummy growl. While exploring, grab a fresh bocadillo (sandwich) or tapas from one of the market kiosks.

Bring Cash: While few merchants take credit cards, cash reigns supreme. Arrive prepared to avoid disappointment.

Grin and Bargain: A warm "Hola" and a grin can go a long way. Don't be scared to haggle for the best deal.

Be Camera Ready: We previously mentioned the photo opportunities, but don't forget to bring your camera! This is a beautiful feast just asking to be photographed.

Local Tapas joint

The tapas scene in Valencia is a colorful tapestry fashioned from tradition, flavor and a whole lot of friendly chaos. Finding the perfect local joint among the innumerable bars and lively plazas, on the other hand, can be like looking for a single grain of rice in a paella pan. Fear not, tapas explorer; this guide will bring you to culinary bliss!

Get Off the Tourist Track

Forget the pricey, cookie-cutter plates that line the main squares. Instead, head into Valencia's heart, where hidden jewels await in quaint backstreets and inconspicuous neighborhoods. Look for locations that are buzzing with local discussion, with the smells of garlic and paprika wafting from their doors, and laughing overflowing onto the pavement. These are the true tapas hotspots.

Accept the Vibe

Each joint has its distinct personality. Is it a darkly lit bodega with old hams strewn about? A boisterous cervecera with wooden tables spilling out onto the cobblestone street? Is a cosy taberna full of vibrant conversations? Allow the ambiance to wash over you, absorb the character, and prepare for a sensory overload.

Small Plates, Big Treats:

Tapas are a feast for sharing, savoring, and debating. Order a few plates at a time, sharing tastes with companions or venturing out on your gastronomic adventure. From the hot kick of "patatas bravas" to the melt-in-your-mouth wonder of "croquetas" in an infinite variety of flavors, to the sizzling symphony of "gambas al ajillo" to the creamy comfort of a "tortilla de patatas," each bite is an homage to Spanish cuisine.

A Salute to Flavour:

No tapa is complete without the ideal beverage accompaniment. Of course, Sangria is a bright must-try, with its fruity sweetness providing a great backdrop to the savory flavors. However, don't be afraid to try local wines, sharp beers, or the refreshing tang of vermouth. Ask the waiters for advice; they're tapas experts who can guide you to the perfect cocktail match.

Getting to Know Your Tapas Paradise:

Become a Local Spy: Tap into the local information of shopkeepers, bus drivers, and even fellow travelers. They'll direct you to hidden jewels and secret areas.

Menus handwritten: on chalkboards or old paper frequently indicate a focus on fresh, seasonal ingredients and traditional recipes.

Follow the aroma trail: The seductive aroma of garlic, paprika, and sizzling meat is a gourmet siren song that will bring you right to tapas nirvana.

Embrace the Unknown: Don't be afraid to step outside of your comfort zone! Order an unknown tapa, be daring with your options, and discover your new favorite flavor.

So put on your walking shoes, explore the backstreets, and let your senses direct you. The ideal local tapas bar awaits, offering an evening of delectable nibbles, shared laughter, and memories that will remain long after the last sip of sangria has been sipped. Have a good day! (Enjoy your dinner!) Now, to personalize this item, please inform me...

- What kind of environment are you looking for? Is it cozy and intimate, lively and bustling, or somewhere in the middle?
- Are there any particular tapas you'd like to try? Traditional patatas bravas, seafood delicacies, or something a little different?

- What is your financial situation? Do you want a splurge-worthy experience or a more laid-back night out?

Valencia's Sweet Treats

The city where the aroma of sizzling paella isn't the only music in the air. The sweetness of local sweets fills the air as well, each mouthful an explosion of flavor and a monument to the city's rich culinary legacy. Let's explore the Valencia delicious delicacies that will have you licking your fingers (and possibly wanting more)!

Classic Appeal

Fartons: The classic Valencian dunkers are this oblong pastry. They're delicious dipped in a glass of creamy horchata (tiger nut milk), with the soft, somewhat sweet pastry giving way to the chilled, nutty drink.

Turrón: This honey, egg white, and almond nougat is a Christmas tradition, but who says it can't be enjoyed all year? There's a flavor for every sweet craving, from basic almond to chocolate-infused.

Bunyols: These bite-sized fritters are available in sweet and savory varieties, with pumpkin and aniseed in the former and cod or prawns in the latter. Put them in your mouth like little bursts of brightness.

Arnad: This cinnamon and lemon zest-infused rice pudding is more than just a treat. It's like a warm hug in a bowl, ideal for chilly evenings or a soothing midday snack.

Modern Variations

Churros with Chocolate: The seductive allure of churros has not been lost on Valencia. But why not add a tasty local spin to them? Dip them not only in melting chocolate but also in creamy horchata for a one-of-a-kind and invigorating experience.

Helado Artesano: It's not simply ice cream here. Artisan gelaterias make small-batch scoops using seasonal fruits and local nuts, as well as adventurous flavor combinations like lavender honey or rose pistachio.

Pastissets de boniato: A hint of autumn enveloped in flaky pastry, these delicious fried pastries are filled with sweet potato jam. They're great with coffee for a cosy afternoon pick-me-up.

Sweet Encounters

Central Market: Take in the sights and sounds of the lively Central Market. Aside from fresh fruit, find local bakeries, honey kiosks, and sellers offering homemade sweets - a sugar lover's heaven.

Horchata Cafeterias: Visit lovely horchata cafes to sample this tiger nut milk beverage. Sip it straight, infused with flavors like vanilla or cinnamon, or with your favorite sweet treat.

Chocolateras: Valencia isn't just about paella and oranges; it's also a chocolate lover's paradise. Discover local chocolatiers who create exquisite sweets from bean to bar, with each taste a delectable homage to chocolate.

Valencia's sweet delicacies have something for everyone, whether you seek classic comfort or modern whimsy. Enjoy the sun, enjoy your senses, and let your inner chocoholic go! A vacation to Valencia isn't complete without a sugar rush, so grab a treat, locate a sunny area, and enjoy the sweetness of this bustling city.

Museum of science Map

Cultural Experience

Festivals and Events

The sun shines as brightly on its exuberant festivals and celebrations as it does on its golden paella and azulejo-tiled buildings. Valencia's calendar is a kaleidoscope of events eager to ignite your senses, from fire-filled fallas to flower-powered clashes, and from art-studded exhibitions to heart-pounding music festivals.

Fire and Fury (March 1st–March 19th)

Fallas, Valencia's undisputed crown jewel, is a pyrotechnic masterpiece unlike any other. Monumental satirical ninots (papier-mâché figures) take over the city, each one providing a humorous or poignant commentary on current events or local personalities. For 19 days, the air is charged with anticipation, culminating in the "Cremà," a stunning night in which the ninots burst into glorious flames, cleaning the city and clearing the way for fresh beginnings.

The Flower Battle of Las Fallas: A Floral Fiesta (the Monday before Fallas)

Prepare for a battle of a different type before the flames take over. During the Batalla de Flores, contesting teams are showered with a perfumed bombardment of carnations. A sea of red and pink petals engulfs the streets, converting the city into a blossoming wonderland.

Valencia International Arts Festival (BIAF): A Stage for the Extraordinary (October)

Calling all art lovers! BIAF brings cutting-edge contemporary performing arts from around the world together. Immerse yourself in the worlds of dance, theatre, circus, and live music, and rediscover the power of artistic expression in all its forms.

The València Grand Fira: A Shopping Extravaganza (July)

Calling all shoppers! The city is transformed into a lively marketplace by La Gran Fira, which showcases the best of Valencian crafts, food, and local enterprises. Discover unique treasures and immerse yourself in the colorful atmosphere of Valencian business, from traditional pottery and hand-woven textiles to gourmet delicacies and craft products.

Valencia Jazz Festival: Let the Music Play (November)

Jazz fans, rejoice! This prestigious event brings together renowned international musicians and upcoming stars to flood the city with the soulful sounds of improvisation and musical magic. Prepare for concerts in historic venues and intimate jam sessions in hidden corners, and let Valencia's rhythm captivate your spirit.

Beyond the Big Names

Valencia's event calendar is a living phenomenon, always presenting something new and fascinating.

Be on the lookout for

Cinema Jove: International Film Festival (June-July) - A cinephile's paradise, featuring indie films, documentaries, and world premieres.

The VLC Basket Season: Support Valencia's beloved basketball team, the Valencia Basket, and immerse yourself in the exhilarating atmosphere of EuroLeague play.

Street art tours: Discover the hidden fact of Valencia's developing street art scene and see the city's walls transformed into bright canvases on street art excursions.

Las Fallas

Prepare to be enthralled by Valencia's most stunning extravaganza - a flaming event unlike any other. Las Fallas presents the city in a colorful tapestry of laughter, critique, and sheer, unadulterated revelry, from towering satirical puppets to deafening explosions. Buckle up, because we're about to dive into the core of this Valencian masterpiece!

A Visual Delight: Ninots Take Over: Forget ordinary monuments; Las Fallas is home to massive papier-mâché figurines known as ninots, which rise like giants across the city. Each is a sarcastic masterpiece, satirizing everything from politicians to pop culture and capturing the Valencian spirit of irreverence and humor. Prepare to be amused, startled, and perhaps even challenged by their witty remarks.

A Colour Riot: Imagine vibrantly colored streets, a funfair of costumes, and buildings draped with colorful banners. Las Fallas is a visual feast in which tradition and spectacle meet in a spectacular show. Take your camera, widen your eyes, and prepare to be dazzled.

Fiery Parties

The Night the City Blazes: The "Cremà," a night of fire that cleanses the city and welcomes new beginnings, marks the culmination of Las Fallas. As night falls, the ninots erupt in flames, lighting the streets in a hypnotic radiance. Witness the show, feel the heat, and allow the rebirth symbolism to wash over you.

Mascletàs: Thunder in the City: Get ready to have your eardrums tickled. The mascletàs are daily pyrotechnic displays that release a sonic onslaught. Cover your ears if necessary, but enjoy the excitement, laughing, and pure exciting pandemonium of it all.

It's Not Just Fire

Flower Power: Witness combat unlike any other in the Batalla de Flores. The city is transformed into a sea of red and pink petals as teams shower each other with a fragrant onslaught of carnations. It's a floral festival, a celebration of beauty and tradition, and an unforgettable event.

A Deeply Rooted Tradition: Las Fallas is a cultural tapestry weaved through generations, not merely a party. Witness traditional dances, listen to the melodies of native instruments, and taste Valencian cuisine. Immerse yourself in the festival's essence and connect with the heart of Valencia.

Tips for Seeing Las Fallas

- Book your accommodations early: This is a popular season to visit Valencia, so make your plans accordingly.
- Wear comfy shoes: You'll be walking a lot, so skip the stilettos and channel your inner explorer.
- Bring earplugs: The mascletàs may be quite loud, especially if you stand close to them. If

you have sensitive ears, please bring earplugs.

- Follow the masses: Following the people is the greatest way to experience Las Fallas. Allow them to direct you to the highlights, hidden treasures, and unique experiences.
- Accept the spirit: Las Fallas is about joy, community, and a shared passion for Valencia. Open your heart, join the party, and let the festival's infectious energy take you away.

Valencia International Film Festival

Valencia, the sun-kissed city where paella sizzles and azulejo tiles dance in the sunlight, also has a thriving film industry! Valencia's film festivals have something for every frame of your cinephile spirit, whether you're a film connoisseur looking for hidden gems or a casual moviegoer looking for a unique experience.

(June-July) Cinema Jove: Where Indie Brilliance Shines

At Cinema Jove, Valencia's international film festival dedicated to new productions and rising talents, immerse yourself in the cutting edge of independent cinema. Explore compelling feature films, thought-provoking documentaries, and intriguing short films from around the world. Discover the next big thing before it hits the mainstream, mix with dedicated filmmakers, and take part in stimulating debates under the summer sky of Valencia.

Away from the Big Screen

Cinema Jove is more than simply a movie theatre; it's a cinematic adventure playground. Attend seminars taught by industry pros, take part in workshops that will help you find your inner auteur, and network with other cinema aficionados from across the world. Discover Valencia's hidden gems on film-themed walking tours, and savor delectable local cuisine at post-screening celebrations.

Embrace the Shadows: The VLC Horror and Fantasy Film Festival (October)

At the VLC Horror and Fantasy Film Festival, dare to enter the realm of spine-chilling shocks and imaginative places. Prepare to scream (joyful terror) as you watch a collection of spine-chilling horror films, strange science fiction, and enchanting fantasy films. From indie nightmares to cult classics, the festival gives known genre favorites as well as emerging voices pushing the bounds of imagination a platform.

Tapas, Camera, Action! A Culinary Cinema Fusion (All Year)

Valencia understands how to combine delicious cuisine with good film. Throughout the year, several venues hold one-of-a-kind events that combine film screenings with gastronomic treats. Enjoy classic flicks beneath the stars with gourmet picnics, dine on themed meals inspired by your favorite films, or attend cooking workshops conducted by celebrity chefs who reveal their culinary secrets inspired by the silver screen.

Tips for Getting Around Valencia's Film Scene:

- Subscriptions to festival mailings will keep you up to speed on programming, special events, and ticket sales.
- Follow the buzz: Look for insider insights and recommendations on local blogs, social media, and online forums.
- Experiment with venues other than the main ones: independent cinemas and cultural centers frequently organize one-of-a-kind screenings and film-related events.
- Accept the linguistic barrier: Don't be put off by subtitles! Many international films are shown with subtitles, introducing viewers to a new world of cinematic experiences.
- Participate in Q&A sessions, workshops, and networking events to fully immerse yourself in the festival experience.

Valencia's film festivals offer an exceptional experience, whether you're looking for worldwide indie jewels, genre-bending thrills, or a cinematic feast for your senses. So, take your popcorn, put on your film reviewer hat, and prepare to enter the colorful world of Valencian movies.

Galleries and Museums

Valencia's museums and galleries offer a feast for the eyes as well as an education for the soul, ranging from ancient artifacts to contemporary masterpieces. So, put down your beach towel for a day and be ready to be wowed by the city's thriving cultural life.

For History Lovers

Valencia's Museo de Bellas Artes: Enter a time capsule of Valencian art, from Gothic splendor to contemporary inventions. El Greco's hauntingly gorgeous paintings, Goya's scathing etchings, and Sorolla's sun-drenched landscapes are all worth seeing. This museum is a love letter to the progress of art that spans decades and styles.

The La Almoina Archaeological Centre: Transports you to Roman Valencia. Explore the ruins of a forum, temples, and baths, and let your imagination run wild through the ancient streets. Interactive exhibitions bring history to life, making it ideal for the time-traveling traveler in you.

The Museo Nacional de Cerámica y de las Artes Suntuarias González Marti: is a magnificent museum where you can get your pottery fix. The collection shows the beauty and workmanship of generations past, ranging from magnificent medieval pottery to delicate Islamic tiles. Be surprised by the complex intricacies and brilliant colors, which are a monument to human innovation throughout history.

For the Contemporary Muse

Instituto Valenciano de Arte Moderno (IVAM): Immerse yourself in the world of modern art at the Instituto Valenciano de Arte Moderno (IVAM). Investigate intriguing installations, provocative artworks, and cutting-edge multimedia exhibitions. Discover new artists alongside well-known ones, and challenge your ideas about what art may be.

Bombas Gens Centre d'Art: This converted factory is a refuge for experimental and inventive art. From video installations to site-specific sculptures, explore temporary exhibitions that push limits and stir conversation. Prepare to be shocked, challenged, and inspired by the sheer creative energy that pervades these walls.

The Centre del Carme Cultura Contemporània, housed in a former monastery, is a nexus for all things modern. There's always something fresh and fascinating going on, from art exhibitions and cinema screenings to concerts and seminars. Take in the creative atmosphere, engage in stimulating debates, and let your artistic spirit fly.

Aside from the Big Names:

Don't pass up Valencia's hidden treasures! Discover tiny galleries nestled away in lovely backstreets, street art covering city walls, and charming art fairs.

You might simply discover your new favorite artist or a hidden classic.

Museum Visiting Tips in Valencia:

- Make a plan: Valencia boasts a diverse collection of museums distributed throughout the city. Determine your main interests and plan your trip appropriately.
- Purchase a Valencia Card: This card provides discounted admission to several institutions as well as public transport, making it an economical way to explore the city's cultural landscape.
- Take advantage of freebies: Many museums provide free admission on specific days or hours. Check the schedules on the websites and arrange your visits accordingly.
- Take a break: visiting museums may be exhausting! Make time for coffee, lunch, or simply sitting and reflecting on what you've seen.
- Make learning interesting and engaging by visiting a museum with interactive exhibits

and educational programs. Don't be afraid to take part!

Natural albufera park

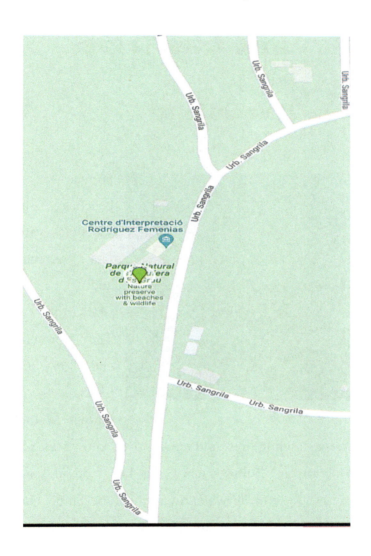

Outdoor Adventures and Day Trips

Beach Vacations

The most popular beaches in Valencia are Las Arenas and La Malvarrosa. The northern end of the beach is known as Las Arenas, while the southern end is known as La Malvarrosa. Both beaches are long, broad, and sandy, with clear water. Swimming, beaching and people watching are all popular activities on this beach.

Patacona: This beach is smaller and less crowded than Las Arenas and La Malvarrosa. Patacona is popular among residents and those looking for a more peaceful getaway. It's also a popular surfing location.

El Saler and La Devesa: These beaches, located in the Albufera Natural Park, are wilder and more natural than the city beaches. El Saler is a pristine beach with dunes and pine woods. The nudist area of La Devesa is right next door.

L'Albufera: A massive lagoon system rich in biodiversity. Boat cruises through the canals are provided, and you can also see migrating birds here.

Pinedo: A long, sandy beach with shallow waters ideal for families with small children.There are several restaurants and bars on the beach.

Port Saplaya: is a modest and picturesque beach with brightly colored buildings and boats.This is a beautiful space to relax and enjoy the scenery.

El Perello: is a peaceful beach with great water. Swimming, sunbathing, and windsurfing are all popular activities.

La Garrofera: is an isolated beach with a lovely landscape. Swimming, beaching and snorkeling are all popular activities here.

La Patacona Sur: A lovely beach with nice water. Swimming, sunbathing, and surfing are all popular activities.

Puçol: is a long, sandy beach with powerful waves. Swimming, beach and surfing are popular activities.

Natural Park of Albufera

Natural Park of Albufera! It's more than a park; it's a biodiversity treasure trove, a tapestry of brilliant colors, and a retreat for people seeking peace in nature's embrace. This watery wonderland, located south of Valencia, invites with its whispering reeds, dazzling lagoons, and countless options for exploration. So grab your binoculars, lace up your hiking boots, and prepare to be amazed by the Albufera's beauties!

A Life Lagoon

Birds of a Feather: With over 300 species calling the Albufera home, it is a magnet for feathered companions. The air is alive with chirps, calls, and the rustling wings of nature's feathered orchestra, from beautiful flamingos striding across the shallows to graceful herons resting on reeds.

A Fishy Tale: A distinct kingdom flourishes beneath the water's surface. Eels, mullet, sea bass, and the strange "samaruc" (Valencian toothcarp) swim among the aquatic plants, giving food for the birds above and a view into the critical environment below.

Rice Fields Refulgent: As the light paints the sky in golden hues, take in the verdant patchwork of rice fields that encircle the lagoon. This landscape, formed by centuries of tradition, not only supplies nutrition but also a spectacular visual treat.Spiritual Adventures:

Boat Tours for the Inquisitive: Glide across the peaceful waters on a "albufera boat," a flat-bottomed watercraft that has crossed these canals for generations. Discover hidden places, spot elusive species, and enjoy the tranquillity of the lagoon from a new perspective.

Secrets of the Trails: Lace up your boots and go off on an adventure through the lush foliage. Follow winding trails to secret lagoons and breathe in the pure air scented with reeds and wildflowers. Each step brings you closer to the Albufera's heart.

El Mirador: A Panoramic Paradise: Climb the observation tower of "El Mirador" and take in the view. The Albufera as a whole spreads out like a gleaming emerald diamond, framed by rice fields and kissed by the sun.

Savoring the Albufera

Paella with a Twist: Try the distinctive "paella de l'Albufera," which swaps regular chicken with soft duck, infusing the dish with the aroma of the lagoon. Every bite is an ode to regional flavors and culinary heritage.

A Squeeze of Citrus: A glass of freshly squeezed Valencian orange juice will refresh your palette. The delicious nectar, filled with flavor and brightness, is the ideal way to toast your Albufera adventure.

Exploration Tips for the Albufera

- Timing is key: Spring and October provide the most comfortable weather and the most vibrant birds.
- Pack of outdoor: Sunscreen, drink, good shoes, and binoculars are vital outdoor companions.
- Respect the Environment: Leave no trace and keep the delicate environment in mind.
- Embrace the Local Charm: Learn about the park's history and traditions at the Racó de l'Olla Interpretation Centre.
- Beyond the Lagoon: Visit El Palmar, a lovely hamlet with traditional eateries and boat rentals.

The Albufera Natural Park is more than just a place to visit; it's an experience. It's an opportunity to reconnect with nature, to observe the wonder of life in all its forms, and to make memories that will last long after you leave its beaches

Sierra Calderona

A verdant country awaits beyond Valencia's sun-kissed beaches and bustling streets. Sierra Calderona, the city's emerald green crown, encourages you to trade cobblestones for forest pathways, and salty breezes for pine-scented whispers. Adventure awaits here, but not in the form of adrenaline-pumping thrills, but in the form of soul-soothing immersion in nature's embrace.

A Singing Landscape

Majestic Mountains: Calderona's summits rise like gentle giants, their slopes cloaked in evergreen forests. Each turn unveils a different scene, sunshine dappling through the leaves and casting shadows on the ancient rocks.

Tapestry of life: Listen to the forest choir made of rustling leaves, avian melodies, and the gurgling murmurs of secret streams in A Tapestry of Life. Inhale the fresh air perfumed with pine and wildflowers, a scent that both energizes and cleanses the spirit.

Secret in the stone: Time has engraved its stories onto the weathered faces of stones, whispering tales of past civilizations and lost paths. Explore hidden tunnels, marvel at the wind and water-sculpted rock formations, and feel the whispers of history touch against your skin.

Every Soul's Path

For the Wanderer's Heart: Lace up your boots and explore the forest's network of trails. Choose an easy stroll through the pines, a more difficult ascent, or simply meander where the route goes, letting the forest guide your steps.

Two Wheels, Two Worlds: Ride along sun-dappled trails with the wind in your hair and the aroma of pine needles in your nose. Discover secluded glades and stunning overlooks while feeling the rhythm of the forest beneath your wheels.

A place for pause: Find a sun-drenched clearing, put out a picnic blanket, and let the forest embrace you. Enjoy the silence, which is only broken by the chirping of crickets and the gentle swaying of leaves. Listen to your inner whispers and reconnect with your inner peace.

A Taste of the Past

Communities with a Smile: Explore lovely communities nestled in the mountain folds. Wander along cobblestone alleyways lined with colorful buildings, eat tapas in sun-drenched plazas, and speak with Valencians whose smiles are as warm as the sun.

Earth's Flavours: Indulge in cuisine made with love and local ingredients. Freshly baked bread, honey poured on goat cheese, and soups simmering with local herbs - each bite is a celebration of the earth and its wealth.

Leaving No Trace and Bringing Memories

Respect this natural haven's fragile equilibrium. Leave no evidence of your presence, walk quietly, and let the forest's murmurs guide you. In exchange, you'll get a calm heart, lungs energized by fresh air, and memories that will remain long after the final rays of the Valencian sun fade.

Pack your curiosity, lace up your boots, and let Sierra Calderona enchant you. This lush paradise awaits, ready to provide a haven for the soul, a playground for the daring, and a whisper of nature's ageless wisdom.

Hiking & Nature Trails

Valencia may be known for its sun-kissed beaches and lively streets, but outside the city boundaries lies a hiking and nature lover's heaven, with a patchwork of verdant trails, craggy mountains, and magnificent coastline walks. Lace up your boots, grab your backpack, and get ready to be transported to the soul-stirring splendor of Valencia's hiking havens.

For the aspiring Mountaineers

Sierra Calderona: The crown jewel of Valencian trekking offers magnificent scenery and difficult climbs. Climb Penyalba, Valencia's highest peak, or discover La Garrofera's secret canyons and old rock formations. Every step reveals a vista of lush valleys and distant azure hues, a prize for every effort.

Chera-Sot de Chera Nature Park: This one-of-a-kind park will take you on a voyage through time and geology. Hike through canyons carved by aeons of wind and water, marvel at prehistoric creature-sculpted rock formations, and uncover secret waterfalls and turquoise pools. Nature exposes its sheer force and beauty during this walk.

For the Leisurely Traveller

El **Saler Natural Park:** Instead of going to the beach, take a walk through El Saler's dunes and pine trees. Follow the paths that wind through the Albufera lagoon, spotting migrating birds among the reeds and inhaling the salty air. This walk is a spiritual balm, a calm study of Valencia's distinct coastal habitat.

Jardines del Turia: This old riverbed has been turned into a beautiful oasis, providing a bit of nature in the middle of the metropolis. Stroll along covered paths, ride past aromatic orange trees, and picnic in the sun. This walk is ideal for a relaxing afternoon away from the hustle and bustle of the city.

Beyond the Well-Traveled Road

El Garb, Ruta Azul: For those looking for a seaside challenge, the Ruta Azul offers a stunning cliffside road from Alboraya to Almenara. Hike along the cliffs, marvel at the roaring waves, and find secret coves and charming fishing communities. This walk exemplifies Valencia's dramatic coastline.

Parque La Canaleta: Explore the depths of the Benagéber mountains to find a secret network of pathways. Explore old water channels, discover secret rock pools, and relax in the peace of unspoiled nature. This walk is ideal for people looking for off-the-beaten-path adventures and hidden treasures.

Hiking Tips in Valencia

- Choose the proper trail: When choosing a walk, keep your fitness level and interests in mind.

- Bring plenty of water, sunscreen, snacks, and appropriate footwear.
- Leave no trace and protect the environment's fragile ecosystems.
- Take in the local flavor by stopping for refreshments in picturesque villages along the way.

Share your adventures by using relevant hashtags on social media.

So put on your hiking boots, grab your map, and let Valencia's paths take you to stunning vistas, hidden treasures, and a restored relationship with nature. It's not only about the goal; it's about the trip, the fresh air in your lungs, and the stories that unfold with each step.

Plaza De La ciudad

Souvenirs and Shopping

Local Markets

Valencia, your beauty goes far beyond sun-kissed beaches and delectable paella. While those charms are apparent, the city's essence may be found in its bustling neighborhood markets. These markets are gateways to local culture, culinary gems, and one-of-a-kind bargains, with bustling halls brimming with fresh produce and picturesque squares ornamented with handcrafted trinkets. So, forego the plan and follow your instincts through a maze of vivid stalls and welcoming people.

A Sensational Feast

Mercado Central: This architectural marvel will leave you speechless. Sunlight pours in through stained-glass windows, lighting mountains of vibrant fruits and vegetables, heaps of gleaming fish, and rows of plump jamón Iberico. The symphony of bartering voices, rhythmic chopping, and the seductive perfume of fresh-baked bread fills the air. It's a sensory feast, a celebration of Valencian richness.

Mercado Colón: Enter a modernist time capsule at this former market-turned-culinary hotspot. Elegant kiosks display handmade cheeses, exquisite chocolates, and exotic spices, while fashionable cafes and tapas bars tease the taste buds. It's a haven for discerning gourmands, where you can linger over coffee and discover gastronomic wonders from all over the world.

Mercat de Russafa: At this neighborhood market, you may immerse yourself in Valencia's bohemian core. Browse stalls brimming with handcrafted items from the area, antique apparel, and upcycled finds. The environment is welcoming and eclectic, with live music frequently filling the air and artists showing their works. It's a soul treasure trove, a place to uncover one-of-a-kind artifacts and drink up the creative energy.

Flea Markets: Explore Valencia's flea markets for hidden treasures and vintage treats. On Sundays, the "Rastro de Valencia" sells antiques, furniture, and collectibles, while smaller neighborhood flea markets like Plaza Redonda reveal varied treasures and local character.

Flower marketplaces: Let your senses bloom at bustling flower marketplaces such as Plaza de la Virgen. Admire the creativity of floral arrangements while inhaling the pleasant aroma of roses, marigolds, and jasmine. It's a bright splash of color against the city's stone walls, a reminder of nature's beauty in the middle of the city.

Christmas Markets: As the year concludes, Valencia transforms into a winter wonderland. Plaza del Ayuntamiento is filled with wooden stalls covered with dazzling lights, selling handcrafted ornaments, local cuisine, and touching presents. It's a magical hideaway, a place to soak up the holiday atmosphere and find the ideal festive token.

Tips for Getting Around Valencia's Market:

- Accept the crowds: Markets are designed to be crowded! Don't be afraid of the boisterous atmosphere; it's all part of the experience.
- Hone your bargaining skills: At flea markets, polite haggling is permitted. Don't be scared to put your Spanish skills to the test!
- Cash is king: Some businesses may not accept credit cards, so bring cash.
- Markets are an excellent opportunity to experience regional delicacies such as horchata or turrón.
- Keep in mind that most markets close by early afternoon, so schedule your trips appropriately.

Fashionable Boutiques

Valencia, Spain's sun-kissed eastern coast city, offers more than simply paella and oranges. It's also a refuge for fashionistas looking for anything more than mass-produced and mainstream items. A bustling network of individual boutiques awaits you in picturesque lanes and stylish neighborhoods. Forget the global chains; these hidden treasures provide one-of-a-kind items, curated collections, and a touch of Valencian flair. So pack your shopping bags and get ready to find hidden gems at Valencia's hottest boutiques:

For the Vintage Collector

SoHo del Carmen: Located in the historic El Carmen district, SoHo del Carmen is a vintage haven. Browse racks brimming with one-of-a-kind items ranging from the 1950s to the 1990s, from delicate flowery skirts to daring biker jackets. The helpful staff is always willing to assist you in finding the ideal piece to add a touch of vintage character to your wardrobe.

Lavespa Roja: Lavespa Roja is a vintage sanctuary specializing in apparel and accessories from the 1920s to the 1970s. Consider gorgeous flapper dresses, stylish pencil skirts, and spectacular jewelry with a tale to tell. Prepare to harness your inner vintage icon and find timeless pieces that will outlast trends.

For the Bohemian Soul

Madame Mim: A delightful boutique bursting with eccentric apparel and accessories, Madame Mim is the place to find your inner muse. Colorful designs and natural materials inspire stories of wanderlust and inventiveness while flowing skirts dance alongside handcrafted jewelry. This is a place for free spirits and those who enjoy the unusual.

Mon Petit Secret: Mon Petit Secret is a cosy boutique tucked away in the Ruzafa neighborhood. The handpicked selection showcases handcrafted apparel, ceramics, and accessories with a distinct bohemian flair by local and independent designers. It's a hidden gem for individuals who value slow fashion and handcrafted creativity.

Minimalist Maven Recommendation

Edit 32: Edit 32 is a refuge of clean lines and refined style. This shop features a carefully curated range of women's clothes and accessories by developing Spanish and international designers.

Consider high-quality fabrics, classic silhouettes, and subtle grace. It's ideal for those who choose quality over quantity and prefer a less-is-more attitude to fashion.

KAIF: At KAIF, a minimalist refuge for both men and women, embrace subtle cool. The clothing on offer is defined by clean lines, neutral tones, and contemporary styles, with a handpicked range of shoes and accessories completing the appearance. It is a destination for folks who value effortless style and things that transcend trends.

Tips for Shopping at Boutiques in Valencia

- Beyond the city center, explore trendy neighborhoods like Ruzafa and El Carmen to find hidden jewels.
- Don't be hesitant to ask for assistance: the personnel at independent boutiques are passionate about fashion and would love to help you locate the ideal piece.
- Embrace the slow fashion movement by taking your time, browsing deliberately, and investing in quality, long-lasting goods.

- Negotiating is acceptable: Don't be scared to bargain pleasantly in some vintage and flea market boutiques.
- Support local designers by shopping at independent stores to support the local fashion sector and discover new talent.

So, avoid the crowds and prepare for a treasure hunt at Valencia's hippest boutiques. These modest havens provide more than simply fashion, with their selected collections, welcoming environment, and hidden gems waiting to be discovered. They give an experience, a chance to interact with the city's creative energy and express your particular style. Have fun shopping!

Valencia unique Souvenirs

Valencia, Spain's sun-kissed eastern coast city, has more to offer than just sunbathers and paella. It's a thriving treasure mine of art, history, and local charm, and what better way to remember your stay than with something more than a fridge magnet? So, bypass the souvenir shops and get into the heart of Valencia to find one-of-a-kind keepsakes that encapsulate the character of the city:

For the Culinary Expert

Paella Spices: Bring a taste of Valencia with you! Purchase authentic paella spices such as saffron, smoked paprika, and rosemary. Share your culinary exploits in Valencia with friends and family back home, and recreate the charm of a flawless paella.

Horchata Concentrate: Enjoy the refreshing sweetness of horchata, Valencia's signature tigernut drink. Buy a concentrate to mix with water and ice, or carry home a bottle of locally made horchata syrup to enjoy a taste of summer sunlight whenever you want.

Turrón: Turrón, a classic Spanish nougat made with honey, egg whites, and almonds, can satisfy your sweet craving. Choose from classic Alicante (hard) to Jijona (soft) flavors and savor the taste of Valencian Christmas magic.

For the Creative Soul

Hand-Painted Ceramics: Valencia is well-known for its thriving pottery history. Purchase a hand-painted tile with classic floral patterns or a one-of-a-kind ceramic dish depicting the city's landmarks. These bright pieces will bring a touch of Valencian warmth into your home.

Silk Scarf: Wear a hand-woven silk scarf to honour Valencia's silk legacy. These exquisitely created scarves are available in a variety of colors and styles, exhibiting classic Valencian patterns as well as contemporary flair. It's a wonderful souvenir that you'll be able to wear and cherish for years to come.

Fallas Figurines: A small figurine can capture the spirit of Las Fallas, Valencia's legendary fire festival. These vividly colored caricatures, which are frequently sarcastic in tone, feature classic festival characters such as "ninots" or "falleras," and serve as a reminder of the city's joyful energy and burning enthusiasm.

For History Lovers

Valencia Vintage Map: Discover a different kind of treasure map! Purchase a historical map of the city that highlights its historic streets and sites. Hang it on your wall as a remembrance of your trips, and let it transport you back in time every time you look at it.

Immerse yourself in the literary tradition of Valencia with a first edition by a Valencian author. Purchase a first-edition book by a well-known Valencian author, such as Vicente Blasco Ibáez or Gabriela Mistral. You'll not only get a one-of-a-kind souvenir, but you'll also obtain a better knowledge of the city's character through its words.

For the Environmentally Conscious Traveller

Locally created Handcrafted Items: Choose sustainably created souvenirs to support local craftsmen while also reducing your environmental imprint. Find gorgeous recycled jewelry, handcrafted bags made of natural fibers, and one-of-a-kind home decor pieces made of wood or ceramics.

Reusable Water Bottle with Valencian Design: Stay hydrated while still being environmentally responsible! Purchase a reusable water bottle with a Valencian design, such as the city skyline, beach views, or traditional patterns. It's a useful souvenir that reminds you of your environmental commitment.

Remember that the finest souvenirs are memories, not items. Explore, discover, and connect with Valencia's dynamic energy. Allow your memento to serve as a physical remembrance of the laughter shared, sights seen, and emotions felt in this sun-kissed city.

Practical Suggestions

Communication and Language

Valencia, Spain's bustling eastern coast city, is enticed with its sun-drenched streets, delectable paella, and contagious enthusiasm. Beyond the postcard-perfect scenery, however, is an intriguing tapestry of languages and communication techniques. So, bundle your cultural curiosity and prepare to negotiate Valencia's distinctive language landscape!

A Tongue Symphony

Valencian and Spanish Dance: While Spanish is Spain's national language, Valencia has its distinct dialect - Valencian. This co-official language of the Valencian Community contains parallels with Catalan but has its melody and lexicon. Don't be surprised if locals sprinkle "bon dia" (good morning) or "gràcies" (thank you) into their Spanish.

English Makes an Appearance: Because tourism is so important in Valencia, encountering English speakers, particularly in key districts and tourist destinations, is rather common. However, excursions into local neighborhoods or interactions with elders may necessitate a few Spanish phrases or hand gestures.

A World of Tongues: Valencia hums with international vibrancy, drawing visitors from all over the world. This melting pot results in a symphony of languages booming through the streets, including French, Italian, German, and even Arabic, giving the city's soundtrack a cosmopolitan flair.

Communication Without Words

Body Language: In Valencia, communication frequently extends beyond spoken words. The discourse includes animated gestures, arched eyebrows, and expressive features. Don't be afraid to mimic this expressive manner - a pleasant grin and an open posture will help you connect with locals.

The Influence of "Siesta": Time moves at a different pace in Valencia. Respect the midday siesta, when companies and shops close for a well-deserved break. Don't expect a quick lunch chat here; conversations are savored and appreciated at a leisurely pace.

Food as a worldwide Language: Eating together is a worldwide language, and Valencia excels in this culinary art form. Food brings people together, transcends languages, and produces lasting memories, from tapas on noisy terraces to private dinners in secluded restaurants.

Learning the Language

While English can get you by in tourist areas, a few basic Spanish phrases like "hola" (hello), "por favor" (please), and "gracias" (thank you) go a long way towards expressing respect and connecting with locals.

Accept-Language Apps: Technology may be your ally! Mobile apps like as Duolingo and Memrise provide bite-sized Spanish courses to help you learn crucial vocabulary and pronunciation techniques.

Immersion: The greatest approach to learning a language is to immerse yourself in it. Start a discussion with a native, listen to Spanish music, or watch Spanish-language films. Accept your mistakes and laugh at your miscommunications; it's all part of the learning process.

Valencia's language and communication techniques are more than just tools; they are intertwined into the city's soul. Understanding and loving its linguistic tapestry allows you to connect more deeply with the people, culture, and spirit of this dynamic Mediterranean gem. So, put your guidebook down, open your ears, and allow the symphony of Valencian tongues to lead you on an incredible experience.

Currency and Money matters

Valencia, Spain's sun-kissed east coast city, greets you with open arms and dynamic vitality. But, before you get carried away by the allure, consider a real necessity: money. The Euro is Spain's official currency, therefore negotiating currency conversion can be difficult. Fear not, brave traveler! This handbook will arm you with the knowledge you need to navigate Valencia's financial landscape:

Understand Your Options

Cash is king: While credit cards are commonly accepted, keeping some Euros in cash is always useful for smaller transactions and unexpected scenarios. However, excessive ATM withdrawals should be avoided due to transaction fees.

ATMs: Numerous ATMs in Valencia accept Euros. To save fees, use bank-affiliated ATMs. Keep your PIN and daily withdrawal limitations in mind!

Currency Exchange Bureaus: These kiosks provide currency exchange, however rates vary widely. Before you commit, compare rates and look for hidden expenses.

Prepaid Travel Cards: Before your journey, load the card with Euros. They provide reasonable exchange rates and avoid ATM fees, but beware of recharge fees.

Invest Wisely

Current Rates: Monitor live currency rates on your phone or on a website such as XE.com. Knowing the current rate can help you spot a good deal.

Avoid Tourist Traps: Avoid currency exchange facilities in high-traffic locations, as they frequently provide unfavorable conversion rates.

Consider Larger Amounts: When it comes to swapping, more is usually better. Exchanging a larger sum frequently results in a slightly better exchange rate.

Prioritise security: by exchanging money only at reputed locations and avoiding street vendors or unwanted offers.

Going cashless

Credit Cards: Because credit cards are frequently accepted in Valencia, they should be considered for larger transactions and restaurants. Be careful of your bank's overseas transaction fees.

Mobile Payments: Contactless payments such as Apple Pay and Google Pay are becoming more common, particularly in larger retailers and restaurants. Check to see if your bank accepts contactless payments.

Helpful Hints

- Inform Your Bank: **Inform** your bank about your travel plans to avoid having your cards restricted due to suspicious activity.
- Always have your passport or ID on hand while exchanging money or using ATMs.
- Learn Basic Spanish: Knowing a few phrases in Spanish, such as "cuánto cuesta" (how much does it cost?) will help you avoid misunderstandings and negotiate better costs.

- Relax and have fun! Navigating Valencia's currency scene will be a breeze with good planning and helpful advice. So enjoy the tapas, explore hidden alleyways, and soak up the Spanish heat. Let the Euros look for themselves!

Health and Safety

Valencia, a sun-kissed city on Spain's eastern coast, is enticed by its vibrant energy, delectable paella, and stunning beaches. However, safety and health considerations must be considered when packing your bags and planning your vacation. Fear not, brave traveler! This guide will provide you with the information you need to travel to Valencia with confidence and peace of mind:

General Security

Minor Theft: Be cautious of your things in crowded areas such as tourist attractions and public transit, as you would in any major city. Use a money belt or safe travel bag to keep valuables near to your body.

Pickpockets: can operate in congested areas, especially during high tourist season. Be extremely cautious when using public transport or walking in congested streets.

Scams: Be wary of popular swindles, such as the "bird droppings" ploy or promises of "unofficial tours." Stick with reputable operators and avoid strangers offering unsolicited deals.

Traffic: While Valencian drivers are generally cautious, remain aware of your surroundings when crossing roadways. Look both ways and use marked crosswalks, particularly in congested areas.

Nightlife: If you want to enjoy Valencia's exciting nightlife, stay in well-lit and busy locations. Inform your hotel or friends of your whereabouts, and refuse beverages from strangers.

Health and Well-being

Sun protection: is essential in Valencia, especially during the summer months. Pack SPF 30 or higher sunscreen and reapply it frequently, especially after swimming or sweating. Protect your head and eyes by wearing sunglasses and a hat.

Hydration: Drink plenty of water throughout the day, especially in hot conditions. Bring a reusable water bottle with you and refill it frequently. Excessive alcohol consumption might exacerbate dehydration.

Food and water safety: Only eat at reputed restaurants and cafes that adhere to appropriate hygienic measures. Avoid street food unless it comes from a reputable vendor. Drink bottled water, especially if you live outside of the city center, where tap water may not be as safe.

vaccines: Before your travel, consult your doctor about necessary vaccines, especially if you are visiting from outside of Europe.

Consider purchasing travel insurance to cover any unforeseen medical expenditures or travel disruptions.

Services for Emergencies

Dial 112: This is the unified emergency number in Spain for all services, including police, ambulances, and fire departments.

Pharmacies: Pharmacies ("farmacias") can be found around the city and are open until late at night. If you want assistance after hours, request "farmacia de guardia."

Helpful Hints

- Learn the fundamentals of Spanish: Knowing a few essential phrases can come in handy in an emergency or when interacting with locals.
- Download emergency apps: For quick access to emergency services and pharmacies, consider downloading apps such as "112 SOS Espaa" or "Farmacias Espaolas."
- Keep up to date: Before your travel, check the local weather forecast and be aware of any potential threats or incidents that could jeopardize your safety.

- Trust your instincts: If something doesn't feel right, get out of the situation and seek help if required.
- You may ensure a safe and healthy visit to Valencia by following these easy rules and using common sense. So bring your sunscreen, bask in the Spanish sun, and enjoy the enchantment of this intriguing city. Remember, a little planning goes a long way towards making your journey worry-free and wonderful!

Hospital

Valencia has a comprehensive network of public hospitals that provide residents and visitors with high-quality healthcare at a reasonable cost. Because each hospital serves different areas and requirements, recognizing their locations and specialties is essential when navigating the city's medical landscape. Let's take a look inside Valencia's public hospitals:

General Hospital:

La Fe University and Politècnic Hospital: This prestigious hospital in Bulevar Sur is the primary center for sophisticated procedures and has various specialized sections including cardiology, oncology, and trauma.

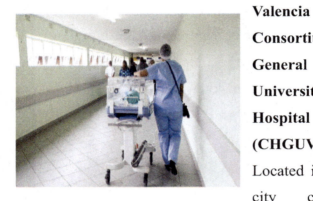

Valencia Consortium General University Hospital (CHGUV): Located in the city center, CHGUV is a big hospital prepared to meet a variety of medical needs. It is particularly strong in paediatrics, neurology, and general surgery.

Hospital Clinic Universitari: Located in the bustling Camins al Grau neighborhood, this prestigious hospital specializes in internal medicine, ophthalmology, and urology. Many people prefer it because of its proximity to the City of Arts and Sciences.

Specialist Hospital

Hospital Malva-rosa: This seaside hospital specializes in rehabilitation and physical therapy and provides novel treatments for musculoskeletal problems and chronic pain. Its location near the Malva-rosa beach gives a tranquil setting for recuperation.

Instituto Psiquiátrico de Valencia: This dedicated facility in Campanar provides mental health treatments to both adults and children. It provides specialized care in areas such as addiction recovery, depression, and anxiety.

Hospital Infantil La Fe: This dedicated children's hospital, located within the La Fe complex, provides all pediatric requirements, from simple checks to complicated surgeries. Its lively ambiance and specialized staff guarantee that young patients have a pleasant experience.

Travel Tip: If you are visiting Valencia and need medical assistance, carry your European Health

Insurance Card (EHIC) or proof of legitimate health insurance with you to expedite access to public healthcare.

Stay Healthy and Have Fun in Valencia!

Valencia's wide network of public hospitals assures your well-being is well-protected. Remember that recognizing your specific needs and utilizing the resources available will lead you to the proper medical care. So sit back and enjoy the Valencian sun, knowing that your health is in good hands.

Conclusion

Your Valencian adventure is waiting for you! This guide has only scratched the surface of this enthralling city. So put down your book, walk out into the sun, and embrace the whirlwind. Get lost in the meandering streets, find hidden gems, and enjoy the beat of Valencian life. Allow your taste buds to dance to the melodies of flamenco, and your heart to swell with the infectious vitality of this intriguing city. Valencia is yours to discover; create your own amazing tale!

Valencia
Travel planner

This planner belongs to

_____

Address:

_____

Date:

_____

My packing list

Documents	Clothes	Personal Care

Tech	Travel	Note

Travel Itinerary

Destination : _____
Duration : _____
Departure : _____
Arrival : _____

DAY 01 — TO DO LIST
08.00 - 09.00
09.30 - 10.00
10.00 - 11.00

DAY 04 — TO DO LIST
08.00 - 09.00
09.30 - 10.00
10.00 - 11.00

DAY 02 — TO DO LIST
08.00 - 09.00
09.30 - 10.00
10.00 - 11.00

DAY 05 — TO DO LIST
08.00 - 09.00
09.30 - 10.00
10.00 - 11.00

DAY 03 — TO DO LIST
08.00 - 09.00
09.30 - 10.00
10.00 - 11.00

DAY 06 — TO DO LIST
08.00 - 09.00
09.30 - 10.00
10.00 - 11.00

MY PACKING LIST

TRIP DATES: _____ / DESTINATION:

clothing & accessories	✔	toiletries	✔
Underwear		Toothbrush	
Socks		Toothpaste	
Bras		Dental Floss	
Sleepwear		Soap	
T-shirts		Deodorant	
Dress Shirts		Shampoo	
Casual Shirts		Conditioner	
Jeans		Hair Brush	
Pants		Styling Tools	
Leisure Shoes		Facial Cleanser	
Hiking Boots		Sunscreen	
Sneakers		Moisturizer	
MISCELLANEOUS	✔	**CARRY-ON ITEMS**	✔
Phone		Travel Pillow	
Laptop/Tablet		Eye Mask	
Film/Memory Card		Earplugs	
List of Medications		Tissues	
Information		Passport	

PACKING CHECKLIST

TRIP DATES: _____ / DESTINATION: _____

CLOTHING & ACCESSORIES	✔	TOILETRIES	✔
Underwear		Toothbrush	
Socks		Toothpaste	
Bras		Dental Floss	
Sleepwear		Soap	
T-shirts		Deodorant	
Dress Shirts		Shampoo	
Casual Shirts		Conditioner	
Jeans		Hair Brush	
Pants		Styling Tools	
Leisure Shoes		Facial Cleanser	
Hiking Boots		Sunscreen	
Sneakers		Moisturizer	
MISCELLANEOUS	✔	**CARRY-ON ITEMS**	✔
Phone		Travel Pillow	
Laptop/Tablet		Eye Mask	
Film/Memory Card		Earplugs	
List of Medications		Tissues	
Information		Passport	

Destination	
Date	
Duration	

DAY 1	DAY 2
DAY 3	DAY 4
DAY 5	DAY 6

Travel Itinerary

Destination : _____
Duration : _____
Departure : _____
Arrival : _____

DAY 01	TO DO LIST
08.00 - 09.00	
09.30 - 10.00	
10.00 - 11.00	

DAY 02	TO DO LIST
08.00 - 09.00	
09.30 - 10.00	
10.00 - 11.00	

DAY 03	TO DO LIST
08.00 - 09.00	
09.30 - 10.00	
10.00 - 11.00	

DAY 04	TO DO LIST
08.00 - 09.00	
09.30 - 10.00	
10.00 - 11.00	

DAY 05	TO DO LIST
08.00 - 09.00	
09.30 - 10.00	
10.00 - 11.00	

DAY 06	TO DO LIST
08.00 - 09.00	
09.30 - 10.00	
10.00 - 11.00	

Destination	
Date	
Duration	

DAY 1	DAY 2
DAY 3	DAY 4
DAY 5	DAY 6

My packing list

Documents	Clothes	Personal Care

Tech	Travel	Note

Printed in Great Britain
by Amazon